Poems for a Soft Mind

Andy Rodriguez

BookLeaf Publishing

Presentation by *BookLeaf Publishing*

Web: www.bookleafpub.com

E-mail: info@bookleafpub.com

ISBN: 9789357448239

First edition 2021

DEDICATION

I want to dedicate these pieces to the friends, family, and loved ones who have kept me sane in such an insane world. You have encouraged me time and time again to put my best foot forward and introduce myself to the world as a poet. I am eternally grateful for your support and will continue to write my heart out in the name of all of you.

ACKNOWLEDGEMENT

People in our lives come and go; I have a multitude of friends and acquaintances that have supported my writing for stretches of time that felt like an eternity. And I spend my days acknowledging that these people ultimately helped shape the poet I am today.

Let’s Travel in a Blue Box

I've spent a life time in the space between planets,
Bouncing around ice-cold comets and lonely rocks.
In my rocket built by heartbreak, I've climbed horizons
And collected dreams left on Saturn's rings.
But then you came in, covered in stardust and life,
Earrings made from galaxies, as your smile shimmered.
You asked to dance around the Universe:
Through Neptune morning hues, delighted and angelic,
And through Mars sunsets, passionate and somber,
Hell, even through Pluto snow, the quietest of white dust.

We continued to dance, through Venus sand beaches

And on each of Jupiter's 79 moons, time danced for us.
Mountains of diamonds on Uranus, luminous as ever,
But only the flicker of a candle in your presence.

Eventually, Earth beckoned to our tired bodies,
Forever embracing the inner home we all seek.
And as Mercury greeted us with a Red Moon all our own,
I admired your serenity as the planets danced around you.

The Truth About Loneliness

Do you ever feel lonely?
Between the oceans of sheets on your bed at the crack of dawn,
sun rays envelope your body whole.
Between the lines in movies,
where teary actors sell stories of love.
And between the stalls in street fairs,
giggles of intimacy fill the air light.

When grasping at thoughts and night terrors
alike, loneliness creeps softly.
On the floor of your mind, an itch
that could never be scratched.
Gaps of still time fill canyon lines;
A plateau incredibly deep, you quiver.
Lost amongst the words of your peers late
Wednesday night,
lonely cocktail glasses litter the tables;
were a moment infinitely stretched,
it would look like an empty train station,
And you're the only one headed anywhere.
Or putting on your favorite outfit

And having nowhere to go.

But the truth is, loneliness can feel like a lot;
Star chasers, car racers, and bread makers,
It sits in the empty spaces between interactions,
quietly attached to your Universe.
And the worst part of loneliness is feeling
like your Universe is the only one in trouble.

The Joy of Running

Life is interestingly similar to running track.
No weight on your back. But you feel it in your feet
Confined to white lines and that's fine.
You accept that your life is good, circulating
Circumstance and baton passes.
With every deep breath, you push forward through
The monotony, a monopoly over your time;
you breathe out and have a second to think,
the lanes do not overlap so should you do the same?
Between rainbows and stars and finish lines,
We're all reaching for our own prize.
But who says there can't be more than one winner
in this lifetime?
So you blast one last song: that graduation song,
That wedding song or even that one karaoke song,
And you sing with everything you've got.
Those thunderous claps wait at the end of this race:
pats on backs, loud hoorays,
And the proudest smile spread across your face.

If I Were to Fall in Love Again

Someone once told me that love comes in
waves.
I want to be whisked away
Just like your favorite morning omelet,
Soft and clear, much like our communication.
Conversation spoken in tongues, traveling light
And lighthearted intention between us.
In daydreams, in city streets, nighttime beats,
The jazz plays for your budding voice
Forever creating a garden of symphonies.
Sandcastle dates, picnics at bordering states,
I packed my heart in the basket beside the wine;
Fruits of affection and sandwiches of promises,
We put on a show and you're always the star.
Communicating through satellites,
You're the Earth and I ride the Sun every day
To forever see you light up those around you.
And I'll kiss you good night as the Moon rises,
Hoping your dreams burst at the seams with
love.
We'll continue to float in endless oceans while

I play my ukulele for you. For you are my serenity
And I want to serenade you so.

Learning to Open up at 28

Spending time with you is like being stranded on a lake.
But in the best way possible for you see:

Centuries of explosive thunder and volcanoes,
From pressures buried underneath layers of human.
Errors and mistakes and regrets written over and over
But never erased from the face.
Release is all the same, powerful and unforgiving,
Like waterfalls and heartbreak calls,
A never-ending communication between nature and soul.

So here we are stranded in this glistening lake,
With water so still, time shines at a freeze.
And I've never wanted to open the door so bad,
For never has anyone looked inside me.

Opened up like textbooks in Autumn,
Highlighted and scribbled, changed so subtly.
It offers fleeting perspective, written all over again,
With the hopes to learn something new successfully.

Hot Air Balloon Ride

Extraordinary, but more extra than ordinary
Is this flight from the past several nights.
Sunset warmth, a glimpse into warmest day,
But more like a play on words, the Jenga way.
My slight move and the trembles become earthquakes,
But your move is musical, the tune to which my body wakes.
The blissful texture of your smile painted in my mind,
Elevated my profound high like a hot air balloon ride.
And as we danced across the continents, toe to toe in sync,
I admired your celestial shape and it forced me to think:

Your silk soft skin woven from distant stardust, and a confidence deemed worthy of ruling the planets.

And as our hot air balloon transcended into space,
we continued to dance among the comets of the unknown.
The beauty of our experience has left me in a daze,
despite being surrounded by Universe noise; we two are alone.
So I take a deep breath and wonder what Heaven you came from,
For the serene aroma of soft homemade kisses escapes your person.
And when our balloon comes down, the adventure isn't done,
in fact it's only just begun, as we embrace this natural immersion.

December 21st

Do you ever feel unfinished?
Like that last piece of birthday cake
Of the day you remember so vividly.
Or perhaps that last drip of coffee
As you get lost in laughter and moments.
Unfinished like that last novel you picked up,
No creases or fingerprints, but forgotten all the same.
Maybe it was that relationship, singing elated tune
But never seemed to leave the station, packed bags still there.
A life long journey that progresses on promises to yourself,
Yet as you cross realms of stars and revelations,
It will always remain unfinished. And much like that quiet fever,
the Winter Solstice embraces the graceful somber of such a word.
Snowfall fills our gloves and our hearts with contemplation,
It slows the engine of our soul.
And on the other end, we come out colorful and jubilant,

For the snow has thawed and so have our thoughts.

Sunday Evening Introspection

We all get put on a path, winding or otherwise,
Filled with a fork or two, especially for you.
But it is not yet complete, you see:
It's missing your mistakes! All of your mistakes,
The ones that remind you to redirect,
Never neglect your inner intellect.
The voice that spells out the hints for you,
Like signs from the Universe, wholly
coincidental.
However, your mistakes are fully intentional.
Beautiful isn't it? However far gone one may
feel,
There's an innate understanding for
Something real. Something home.
And we create a home out of the stars we
capture,
the moons in our orbit. The celestial rings,
decorated with experience and things.
So cheers to all of your mistakes, the ones that
lead
us astray, that lead us away, even lead us to stay.

Those are the ones that remind us to move,
remind us to hurt, and remind us to love.

What's For Breakfast?

Noticeably slow everything moves,
Waking up to the sound of your voice.
"Good morning sunshine," in elated tune,
"I've got something in store for you."
And as the World turned, your doofy smile shined
The space surreal, our home away from timelines.
In the kitchen we convened, it smelled like adolescence,
like blueberry pancakes in the Summer. Like love.
Our table, memories scratched in, set for two
As we delve into the Seasons of me. Seasons of you.

Gales of Autumn, asteroid belts of leaves,
Bright colors lighten new passionate evenings.
While Winter silence brought comets of excitement,
Elliptical and consistent, eternally blissful.

Spring sounds like affection blossoms,
Like flower beds and soft baked breads.
Full revolution we come, the Summer of our escape,
To the end of problems, a new planet to which we lay claim.
"Of all the seasons, I like yours all the more,"
Expressed I with a doofy smile of my own,
"Within you contained, an entire Universe unknown,
One I honestly cannot wait to explore."

A Contemplative Universe

Shooting stars burn up inside of your
atmosphere,
With a beautiful mind and hard thoughts in good
measure,
the sun sets on your horizon and yellow hues
mellow the world,
for the conversations you hold close,
are the most intimate pleasure.

Comets and meteors crater your surface,
but under that soft exterior lies an angel among
books,
fiction, fantasy, a living embodiment
of everything dreamy and whole,
Til' the end is reached, embracing how the new
world looks.

And with revolutions complete:
You fall off the edge of the galaxy,
ready for new adventures among exploding
giants and belts,

you begin a new story, a new galaxy, new lights,
new stars,
But blissfully under a bigger sun, embracing
your heart before it melts.

Constellations of Conversation

An enormous carafe of knowledge,
strung across the constellations.
Of facts, of rhythms, of unknowns.
He embraced the complexity of an asteroid belt,
All the while lost in his comet's trail.
Tall and slightly abashed,
Nothing gleaming or unseemly,
But much like the moon, always beaming
even when he has to share the sky with the Sun.
On a trail of never ending spectacles,
through clouds and atmospheres,
never holding on to his fears,
until he figures out the place he can call home.
And home never looked so close,
for as he looked down at the solar system,
he saw one final constellation:
A clue that led him to ever-lasting joy.

Adoration for Simplicity

An intimacy unknown in this world,
Like the clattering of old wooden chairs,
Peeling off the outer insecurities
While we delight in even the slightest stare.
It was crowded, but a caterpillar's distance away
From the next closest Galaxy, just you and me
And the stars we choose to shoot across Space.
Intimacy like the landscape of Antarctica,
Quiet and untouched but intricate in design;
Cold and elegant, hugging across the surface,
Underneath, a molten core that melted my
frozen heart.
Stillness in my adoration, loud laughter in
Constellations,
In this Galaxy of conversation of new found
passion.
She smiled at me and the Sun imploded,
And as the cascading warmth created a new
system,
I proceeded to rewind and have another listen.

A beautiful intimacy in quiet words spoken,

In this home of stars and comets and beauty.
Clinks of glass to celebrate time's past,
And acknowledge that there a ways to go.

If Ever Did I Ever

If I've ever had a second to think about this,
The discrepancies and disparities,
the love for me and how I adore thee,
between family and living care free,
around the galaxy, searching wildly,
for every universe lovely like dense shrubbery,
the carve in every tree, locks of hair so sweet,
and enticing glee, what a beautiful memory.

Like the opening of a new book,
A fresh adventure hidden amongst letters,
To u, to i, all the trading of tears and smiles,
The open road with more than one turn darkened
Until the end, the sky opens up with yellow
hues,
We paid our dues, and that book closed on a
blank cover.

Much ado about the rough sea, turning tides,
Turning fleeting sheep into hardened wolves,
Turning haunting guise of missed lovers,
surrounded by
The woes of lonely creatures and their fevers,
Hunting for love under the world, running out of
time.

A playful sandbox, mountains of sand to climb,
And buckets of kisses lay on my cheek.
A desert not five meters wide, you're my Oasis,
An undeniably lush atmosphere, complete
With your smile and beautiful hands.
But the wind blew our sandcastle away.

For if I've ever had a second to think of you,
and the things you do, morals you hold onto,
it becomes so bittersweet, like unripened fruit,
for you remind me of a time so simple and true.
And if these were my last few moments to think,
If ever,
did I ever,
Love you for being you.

Simply Expressed

Poetry, in it's rawest form
Is but an extension of one's dreams,
Spread across paper canvas
Or photography on flimsy film reels.
Painted across a page, artistry
Relatable, tangible, and achievable
Like overcoming that impossible crush
Or even a fish of rainbow scales.
The ingenuity of it all, hearts stable.
Like the hug from a close friend,
it is something quietly appreciated
And vulnerability unwound, no words
But a silent bond between you and them
Beautifully remediated.

This is poetry in it's rawest form.
Embracing simple memory in verse
Until emotion comes to explosion,
And your stars align in the Universe
Of self discovery.

Born to be a Model

Being a model isn't just physicalities,
But born with a heart of steel, pulsating
Through harshest of common brutalities
With a goal in place to build a kingdom.
Finding a home among the few,
A forest of fruitful, fortified friendship,
And among memories of what you do
Forever imprinted the beauty of your home.
The Model learned to be like water,
Patient, understanding and deep.
An incoming shooting star, you grow hotter,
And create a crater of your love.
And you've never given up, have you?
Rising like the wistful hot air balloon,
Floating to blue, maybe something new,
Waiting for the day you finally get to rest.

And you remember that lullaby, you remember it well.
When Mother Goose would put you to bed,
Reminiscing of the day from Heaven you fell,
And into the arms of this precious world.
An ode to you, a toast to life,
No hindrances for the Model in disguise.
For the honest woes, you take in strife,

Are reminders to you that you've only just
begun.

What Makes a Home?

What makes a home away from home?
Is it the way the walls bring life to space,
or the way simple arts speaks to the people?

Tiles rearranged in mosaic pleasure,
like those of a fine Egyptian rug tucked away,
or stools that remind you of hidden basement bars,
complacently unused but taking space anyway.

Friendly faces attached to new conversation,
like bloomed plants reaching for your chin,
or the laugh of an inside joke being passed along,
from the windows to the hand-me-down couch within.

Shelves filled with memories of pick-me-ups,
little wrapped favors of personal connection,
Remind you that a place so far from your own home,

can fill a heart with such profound affection.

So come on in, pleasure will follow right behind
you,
the aroma of a good coffee with a pump of better
times,
grab a cup, sit down and get to know a friend,
for these are going to be the best moments of our
lives.

Waiting for Friday Sunset

Complacent,
You sit still, counting down minutes, hours, days.
Wishful realities force mid-afternoon haze,
And you wonder,
Where does the time go?
Screeching rails of a departed train,
Our dreams packaged like cargo, tight and similar,
We can't point out which is ours.
We've disappeared into the lives of others,
Forever hoping to catch a glimpse,
"To be alive," they call it, but a feeling we only Observe.

It's Friday and you smile,
For the next 48 hours you dedicate to purpose,
To adventure, to living freely outdoors,
Like a bird, wings spread and never too tired to fly.
But why? Why not fly every day?
The measure of a bird is not in its wingspan,

But its willingness to fly, whenever it can.
For every day is a brand new day, better or worse,
At an altitude, fearful at first, forces new comfort.
So embrace yourselves and all you're worth everyday,
For you learn to live life uniquely in every single way.

Glistening Under the Neon Lights

Lead us not into perfectionism,
But deliver us from our insecurities.
An absolutely stunning view of purity,
Beloved intention, the strongest is fury.
Or passion? The lounge music is mashin'
And I'm not understanding the fashion.

Hearts dance under lights, spotlight veins.
A discontented beat when the groove is off.
Is the groove off?
A heart has two beats not in sync so is one
Ever really off?
We live the night away hoping to wake in
Far away places, with mysterious faces.
A symbolic collection of social races but
Could you ever really win every single one of
them?

So in the middle of Tokyo, I embrace you.
And the signs buzz on cue, what an extravagant
view
Glistening under the Neon light.

And as we get lost in mazes of
miscommunication,
Language slips but our hearts click
In alleyways of unspoken keepsakes.

An Evening in a Cave

I've always wondered why water glistens,
In the darkest of hours and without the Moon.
Searching the Earth and enticing islands afloat,
The isles between my heart and mind are full,
But the water doesn't glisten.
So I decided to spend an evening in a cave,
Covered in dark and conversing with the bats.
A stillness overcame me, swimming in that
space.
Between the ends of perfection and
imperfection,
I realized exactly why there's a glistening inside.
Despite the ebbs and flows, water just is.
And so is the grass, the tides, and even life;
Translated into quiet but momentous
experiences.

You make me feel like water,
Beautifully still and undeniably translucent.
For you are the light I've let in,
And that scares the darkest parts of me.
Of what just is no longer will be.

My Summer in Sunlight

Here I float in the middle of a beautiful Summer day,
Daydreaming within my Japanese pop playlist;
I see you in divine shade under your parasol,
Brightly decorated in deep red and peach flowers.
And as guitars whine in my ears, my heart thumps
As it begins to play out our story, velvety and short.
You hide under that parasol like a turtle,
Soft in the center like a finely crafted tres leches;
Your eye shadow so inviting and a heart all alone
But already thumping to the next song in my playlist.
I rock my head to electrifying tracks but I imagine
Your inviting smile and eyes, quiet and telling.
So I take this opportunity to experience your parasol;

The warmth of the sun with the depth of an ocean,
Swallowed no longer by my music, but by you.
And this short-lived memory reminds me of purity:
The beauty of falling in love with someone special.

So dedicate a song for your loved one,
The Guardian Angel forever keeping you safe and loved:
That way each time the drums beat and pianos ring,
Your body rocks to the tune of their memory.

A Holiday All Your Own

You're as quiet as snow.
Warm and sweet like Christmas hot chocolate,
You float in my mind just like those
marshmallows.
Fluffy dreams of waking up next to you,
I concede defeat, you've stolen my heart.
You gift wrap pieces of it and give it back in
bits,
Cinnamon kisses and all, how soft of you.
Blissfully soft like Grandma's pumpkin pie,
You're easy to enjoy and hard to forget.

Through brisk Winter nights, the wind blows
My thoughts wayward. But you stay there.
Just like those golden ornaments, I'm hooked.
And you compliment my empty, branched
facade;
Decorated with fairy lights and silver wings
alike,
You prepared me to put on a show for all to see.

And I think I'm ready to love you,

But first I have one final gift perfectly wrapped.
Playing with words, I’ve strung some together,
To create an image of you, Heavenly soft.
And along with chestnuts and candy canes,
Minty-aired lines to mellow out your pains.
So open up my heart, tangled veins and all,
And let’s spend a timeline celebrating your
holiday.

www.ingramcontent.com/pod-product-compliance
Lightning Source LLC
Chambersburg PA
CBHW051745130826
49812CB00033B/1006
* 9 7 8 9 3 5 7 4 4 8 2 3 9 *